Easy Steps

1 Bend.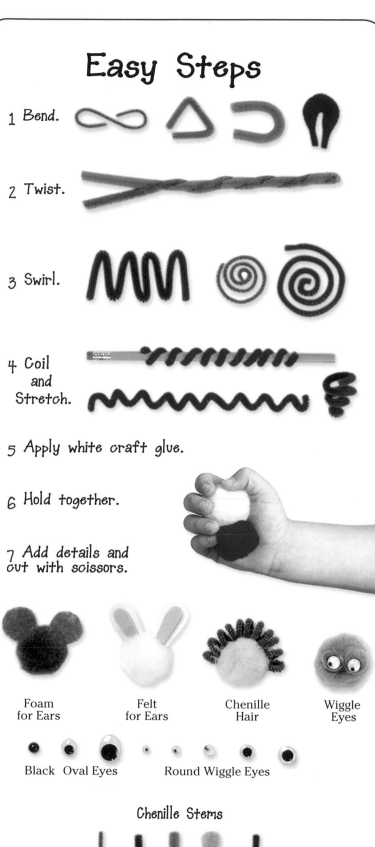

2 Twist.

3 Swirl.

4 Coil and Stretch.

5 Apply white craft glue.

6 Hold together.

7 Add details and cut with scissors.

Foam for Ears

Felt for Ears

Chenille Hair

Wiggle Eyes

Black   Oval Eyes   Round Wiggle Eyes

Chenille Stems

3mm

Cute Pencil Toppers

Bumble Bee - PomPoms (Black 1½", 2 Yellow 5mm), Chenille stems (White bump, Yellow 6mm, Black 3mm), Pencil, Two 6mm wiggle eyes

Bookworm - PomPoms (Red 1½", 2 Green 10mm), Green 6mm chenille stem, Green and Brown Foam, White paper, Two 4mm wiggle eyes, Pencil

Sunflower Pencil Topper - PomPoms (Brown 1", six Yellow ¾", 5 Green 5mm), Green 3mm chenille stem, Green Fun Foam, Pencil

Playful Puppets

Get together with friends on a rainy day to make a whole ZOO!

Tom Cat - PomPoms (1" Yellow, 2 White 10mm, 5mm Pink), Chenille stems (Yellow and Orange 6mm), Two 5mm wiggle eyes

Mouse - PomPoms (1" Grey, 10mm Grey, 5mm Pink), Pink and Grey felt, Two 5mm wiggle eyes

Fluffy Bunny - PomPoms (1" White, two 10mm White, 5mm Pink), Chenille stems (White bump and Pink 6mm), Two 5mm wiggle eyes

Big Black Spider - PomPoms (Black - 2", 1", eight 10mm; Green 10mm), Three Black 6mm chenille stems, 2 Black 6mm half round eyes, White Fun Foam, Red knit glove

Curly Lion - PomPoms (1" Yellow, two 10mm Yellow, 5mm Black), Two Orange 9mm chenille stems, Two 5mm wiggle eyes

Ted E. Bear - Pompoms (1" Dark Brown, two 10mm Dark Brown, 1/2" Beige, 5mm Black), Two 5mm wiggle eyes

Elephant - PomPoms (1" Pink), Pink bump chenille stem, Pink and Grey felt, Two 5mm wiggle eyes

Puff, the Dragon - PomPoms (Green - 1", 1/2", Yellow two 5mm), Purple and White Fun Foam, Two 5mm wiggle eyes

Elsie Cow - PomPoms (1" Black, two 3mm Black, 1/2" Pink), White 6mm chenille stem, White and Pink Fun Foam, Two 5mm wiggle eyes, Small cow bell

Fido - PomPoms (1" Beige, 10mm Black), Brown 15mm chenille stem, Red felt, Two 5mm wiggle eyes

Spot the Dog - PomPoms (1" White, 10mm Black), Black bump chenille stem, Red and Black felt, Two 5mm wiggle eyes

Let's play cat and mouse! Eeek...

SPOT DOG

TOM CAT

MOUSE

FLUFFY BUNNY

CURLY LION

Roar!

TED E. BEAR

I never forget!

ELEPHANT

PUFF DRAGON

ELSIE COW

FIDO D...

Felt Body
Cut a 2 1/4" felt square and trim bottom edge with pinking scissors. Sew gathering stitch on top edge, pull tight and tie off. Glue open sides together. Glue head on body.
Glove Body
Glue heads on glove fingertips.

FRAME

Make a magnetic frame for mom, dad, grandmom, teacher and everyone else on your list! A cute frame makes a perfect gift with your latest school photo inside.

And they are great with a special message.

Mouse - PomPoms - (1" Grey, 10mm, Yellow, 5mm Pink), Chenille stems (Pink 3mm and Hot Pink 6mm), Grey and Pink felt, Two 5mm wiggle eyes, White and Yellow Fun Foam, White paper, Magnet strip, $\frac{1}{4}$" hole punch, Black marker
INSTRUCTIONS: Cut foam pieces using pattern and punch holes in Yellow piece. Write 'Say Cheese' on paper. Assemble mouse and flag, glue on frame. Glue magnet on back.

You can never have enough photo frames, and you can never have too many magnets! Create magnetic frames to tickle your fancy!

Some Bunny Loves You - PomPoms - (White - 1", two $\frac{1}{2}$", two 10mm; Orange - $\frac{3}{4}$", $\frac{1}{2}$", 10mm; Pink 5mm), Chenille stems (Hot Pink 6mm, Pink 6mm, Green 6mm, White bump), Two 5mm wiggle eyes, Pink and Yellow Fun Foam, White paper, Black marker, Magnet strip, $\frac{1}{4}$" hole punch
INSTRUCTIONS: Cut foam pieces punch holes from Yellow piece. Glue holes and Hot Pink chenille on frame. Assemble bunny and carrot, glue on frame. Write 'Some bunny loves you' on paper, glue behind opening. Glue magnet on back.

Ladybug Love - PomPoms (Red 1", 2 Black $\frac{1}{2}$", 4 Red 5mm, 14 Black 3mm), Chenille stems (Black and Green 3mm), Four 4mm wiggle eyes, Purple Fun Foam, Magnet strip
INSTRUCTIONS: Cut foam pieces using pattern. Assemble 2 ladybugs, glue bugs and grass on frame. Glue magnet on back.

Cat & Mouse - PomPoms (Black - 1$\frac{1}{2}$", 1"; White - 1", three 10mm; 2 Pink 5mm, 13 Light Blue 5mm), Chenille stems (Black 6mm and Pink 3mm), White and Pink felt, Four 5mm wiggle eyes, Purple and Pink Fun Foam, Magnet strip
INSTRUCTIONS: Cut foam pieces using pattern. Glue Light Blue PomPoms around opening. Assemble mouse and cat, glue on frame. Glue magnet on back.

Baby Doll

Create a huggable little doll with a glove, and make her baby too.

PomPoms - (Pink - 1½", two ¾"; Light Blue ¾"), Knit glove, 2" of ½" scalloped lace, Two 4mm and two 6mm wiggle eyes, Earring back, Safety pin, Polyester fiberfill, Needle and thread

Glove - Cut glove as shown. Use hand for main body, cuff for hat and thumb for baby blanket. Apply glue to cut edges to prevent raveling.

Body - Glue thumb edges together. Sew gathering stitch at top, lightly stuff body, pull stitches tight and tie off. Glue lace for collar. Glue large Pink PomPom for head. Glue 6mm eyes and earring back pacifier in place.

Hat - Sew gathering stitch at top and bottom. Pull top tight and gather bottom to fit head. Glue hat on head and Light Blue PomPom on hat.

Baby - Glue remaining PomPoms together. Glue 4mm eyes on head. Cut small slit in thumb and glue baby in place and add safety pin.

Happy Hats

Spider Hat - Four 1" Black PomPoms, Four Black 6mm chenille stems, Eight 6mm wiggle eyes, Red baseball cap, Glue

Finger Rings

Bumble Bee - PomPoms (1" Black, two 5mm Yellow), Chenille stems (Black 3mm and Yellow 6mm), White felt, Two 6mm wiggle eyes, ¼" elastic

Blue Lady Bug - PomPoms (1" Light Blue, ½" Pink, five 5mm Yellow), Pink 3mm chenille stem, Two 4mm wiggle eyes, ¼" elastic

Bookmarks

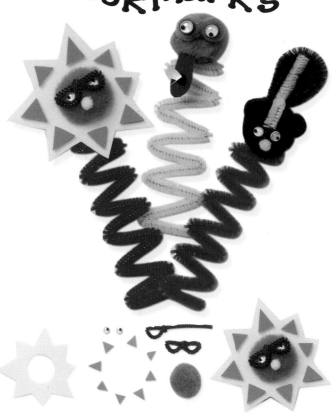

Don't worry... Be Happy! You'll love making and wearing these clever caps. Make one in every color, to match any outfit.

Ladybug Hat - PomPoms (Red - seven 1", ten 5mm; Black - five 10mm, thirty-five 3mm), Chenille stems (Black 3mm and 6mm), Ten 4mm wiggle eyes, White baseball cap, Glue

Sunshine - PomPoms (1" Orange, 5mm Yellow), Chenille stems (Blue 3mm and Red 6mm), 5mm wiggle eyes, Yellow and Orange Fun Foam

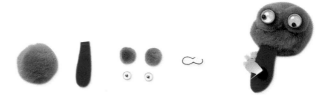

Freddy Frog - PomPoms (Green - 1", two 10mm, Black - 5mm), Yellow 6mm chenille stem, Red felt, 6mm wiggle eyes, White paper

Stinky Skunk - PomPoms (Black - 1", two 10mm; Pink 5mm), Chenille stems (White and Hot Pink 6mm and Black bump), 6mm wiggle eyes

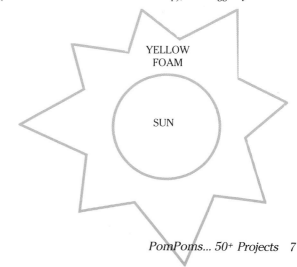

YELLOW
FOAM

SUN

Springy Shoes

Get your friends together and have a sneakers party to dress up those drab white tennies. You will have great fun!

Butterfly Tennie - Six 10mm Orange PomPoms, Chenille stems (Two Pink bump and two Purple 3mm)

Bear Buddies Tennies - PomPoms (Beige - four 1", eight 10mm; White four ½"; Black four 5mm), Two Pink 6mm chenille stems, Eight 5mm wiggle eyes, Two ½" Pink ribbon roses
NOTE: Make the bear heads beige or brown.

Tiny Creatures

Be a better bug catcher! These cuddly little furry critters don't ever bite or sting. They are friendly fellows who make good pets for everyone.
Mom will like them too!

Frog - PomPoms (1½", 1" and two 10mm Green; 5mm Black), Green 6mm and bump chenille stems, Red felt, Two 6mm wiggle eyes, White paper

Snail - PomPoms (Two ½" Blue), Purple 6mm and Red 3mm chenille stems, Pink Foam, Two 5mm wiggle eyes

Coil Chenille stem around pencil for tennies.

Pink & Green Tennies - Four ¾" Yellow PomPoms, Chenille stems (Two Green 6mm and two Hot Pink 6mm)

Pompom Tennies - 10mm Red, Orange, Yellow and Green PomPoms to fit around shoes, Two Red 6mm chenille stems

Make a Sneaky Snake and a Giggly Gecko...

Green Snake - 1" Green PomPom, Chenille stems (Red 3mm and 3 Green 15mm), Two 6mm Black half round eyes

Worm & Apple Frame - PomPoms (Red - 1", two 5mm; Black eight 5mm;   Green six 10mm), Chenille stems (Green 3mm and 6mm), Green, Yellow and Black Fun Foam, Two 5mm wiggle eyes, Pinking scissors

Crazy Critters are fun to make for all ages.

Make dozens to decorate your walls, your room and your locker at school.

"My refrigerator is covered... front and sides with special mementos from my children."

Suzanne

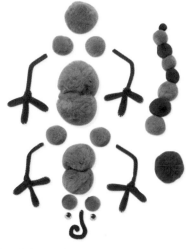

Blue & Green Gecko - PomPoms (Green - two 2", three 1½", six 1", four ¾"; Blue 1½", 1", two ¾", 10mm), Chenille stems (Red 6mm and 4 Blue 6mm), Two 10mm wiggle eyes

This and That

Get together with your friends to see who can create the NEATEST little accessories.

You can even have 'Trade Day' gifts and projects.

At your next party or group meeting, ask your Mom to bring the PomPoms and supplies... then you can have all the fun!

Crazy Critters

Walk along, hop about, swing from a vine or clippity clop... create a whole ZOO!

Flamingo - PomPoms (Five 1½" Pink), Chenille stems (Pink 15mm, 4 Hot Pink 6mm, Yellow bump, 2 Pink bump), Two 10mm wiggle eyes

Tree Frog - PomPoms (Four 1½", two ¾" and twelve 10mm Green), Chenille stems (Red 6mm, 4 Green 6mm, Green 15mm, Green bump), Two 10mm wiggle eyes

Monkey - PomPoms (Brown - three 1½", two ½"; Beige - ¾", two 10mm), Chenille stems (4 Brown 15mm, Brown 9mm, Yellow 3mm, Yellow bump), Beige felt, 5mm Black half round nose, Two 6mm wiggle eyes

Twisted Snake - PomPoms (1" Green), Chenille stems (3 Brown 15mm, 3 Green 15mm, Red 3mm), Two 5mm Black half round eyes

Sheep - PomPoms (1" and ten ¾" White; ¾" Black), Black 6mm chenille stem, Black and White Foam, Small brass brad, 6mm wiggle eye
INSTRUCTIONS: Cut body from White and legs from Black foam using patterns. Assemble sheep referring to photo.

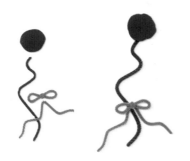

Terrific Cards

Create a handmade card. Fun and easy!

Balloons Card - PomPoms (Yellow, Orange and Red 1"), Chenille stems (Dark Blue and Orange 3mm), White paper, 8½" x 11" piece of Purple cardstock, Black marker, Scallop scissors

Going Batty Card - PomPoms (Two 1" Black, four 5mm Yellow), Chenille stems (Black 3mm and 9mm, White 3mm), Black Fun Foam, 6" x 11" piece of Orange cardstock, Pinking scissors

BOO! Card - PomPoms (2" and 1½" Orange), Chenille stems (Black 3mm and 6mm and Green 6mm), Black Fun Foam, 5½" x 11" piece of Green cardstock, Pinking scissors

Snowman Card - PomPoms (White - two 1", ³/₄", ½"; Yellow three 5mm; Green 5mm; Red 5mm; Black 5mm), Chenille stems (Orange 6mm, Black and Brown 3mm), Black felt, White and Yellow Foam, 8" x 4" piece of Red cardstock, Pinking scissors

Happy Holidays Card - PomPoms (Three ½" Red), Green Foam, 9¼" x 4³/₄" piece of Green cardstock, 4¼" square of White paper, Pinking scissors

Reindeer - PomPoms (Beige - two 2", 1½", 1"; Black - four 1", 10mm; Dark Brown ³/₄"), Chenille stems (2 Brown 9mm and 2 Brown 3mm), Brown Fun Foam, Two 6mm Black half round eyes

Birthday Cake Card - PomPoms (Three ½" Yellow and eight 5mm Light Blue), Chenille stems (Purple, Orange and Red 6mm), Pink and White Fun Foam, 10½" x 6" piece of Blue cardstock, Scallop scissors

BOO! Card Patterns and instructions on page 13.

Don't miss out... on a single fun and fabulous PomPom creation. You'll have a great time creating everything from clowns to critters, from snakes to friendly faces!

Simply glue PomPoms together with white craft glue. Your Mom can help you by using a hot glue gun to make gluing faster.

Either way, you're sure to brighten every day with lots of fun and friendship!

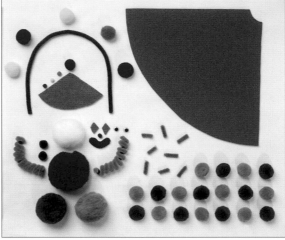

POP-UP CLOWN
CONE
RED FOAM

Pop-up Clown - PomPoms (Red - 2", two 3/4", 1/2", two 5mm; Yellow - two 3/4", 5mm; Orange - 3/4", 5mm; Green - 1 1/2", nine 3/4"; Blue - two 10mm, 1 1/2", nine 3/4"; White 1 1/2"), Chenille stems (Purple, Blue, Red and 2 Green 6mm), Purple and Orange felt, Two 8mm wiggle eyes, 1/4" dowel, Black and White acrylic paint
INSTRUCTIONS: Cut hat and eyes from felt and cone from foam using patterns. Assemble clown and cone as shown. Paint dowel White, dot Black. Glue clown on dowel. Insert dowel in cone.

CLOWN HAT
PURPLE FELT

Pop-Up Clown

Small Clown - PomPoms (Red - 1", 5mm; White 3/4"; Green 10mm; Dark Blue - two 10mm, two 5mm; Yellow two 10mm; Black 3mm), Chenille stems (Purple, Green and Red 3mm), Red felt

Pompom Fun!

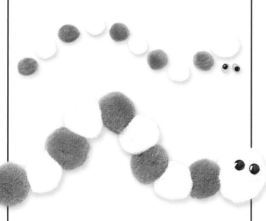

Worm - PomPoms (1" and four 3/4" Yellow, five 3/4" Green), Two 7mm x 10mm oval wiggle eyes

Chick - 1 1/2" Yellow PomPom, Chenille stems (Yellow bump and Orange 6mm), Orange felt, Two 6mm Black half round eyes

Skeleton

Hang 'Scary' on a spring from an old spiral notebook to make him bounce.

Scary Skeleton - PomPoms (White - 2", 1 1/2", twenty 1"; Yellow two 1/2"; Black two 5mm), Chenille stems (6mm Black and two 6mm White), Small plastic spider, Spring from a spiral notebook
INSTRUCTIONS: Cut 1" piece of White chenille for neck and remaining White chenille into 1 1/2" pieces. Assemble skeleton as shown. Cut Black chenille to make mouth as shown. Glue Black PomPoms on Yellow PomPoms for eyes, glue on head. Glue spider on chest.

Tic·Tac·Toe

Create a clever little game! Use colorful PomPoms and drinking cups.

Tic-Tac-Toe Game - PomPons (Yellow - five 1 1/2", ten 5mm; Orange - five 1 1/2". ten 5mm), Chenille stems(two Black 3mm and two Purple 6mm), Twenty 10mm x 15mm oval wiggle eyes, 9 styrofoam cups, Purple paint, Paintbrush, 1/4" hole punch

Fantastic Necklaces

Spark up your jewelry!
Make COOL hair accents, necklaces and little dolls.

Yellow Lady Bug - PomPoms (1" Yellow, ½" Light Blue, five 5mm Pink), Chenille stems (Pink 3mm), Two 4mm wiggle eyes, ¼" elastic

Friendship Doll Necklace
Blue Doll - PomPoms (¾" White, 1" and ten 10mm Light Blue), Yellow 3mm chenille stem, Two 5mm wiggle eyes, 1½" of ⅝" lace
Pink Doll - PomPoms (¾" White, 1" and ten 10mm Pink), Brown 3mm chenille stem, Two 5mm wiggle eyes, 1½" of ⅝" lace
Yellow Doll - PomPoms (¾" White, 1" and ten 10mm Yellow), Orange 3mm chenille stem, Two 5mm wiggle eyes, 1½" of ⅝" lace
Necklace - Two Pink bump chenille stems

Make Gifts for Friends and Family!

Bunny & Chicks

Create a cute favor or table decoration with Pompoms and a Tuna Can.

Bunny's Can of Chicks - PomPoms (White - 1½", twelve 1", two ¾"; Pink 10mm; Yellow twelve 1"; Orange - 1", ¾", 10mm), Chenille stems (Green and Orange 6mm, White and Hot Pink bump), Two 10mm and twenty-four 4mm wiggle eyes, Purple Fun Foam, Orange felt, Tuna can

Carrot - PomPoms (Orange - ¾", ½", ¼"), Chenille stems (Green 6mm), INSTRUCTIONS: Assemble carrot, glue.

Photo Bracelet or Watch - PomPoms (ten 10mm Green and fourteen 5mm Red), Two Blue 6mm chenille stems, Blue Fun Foam, Photo

Heart Necklace - PomPoms (eight ³⁄₄" Red and eight ³⁄₄" Pink), Red bump chenille stem, 16 Purple pony beads, Red embroidery floss, Needle

Cool Bracelets

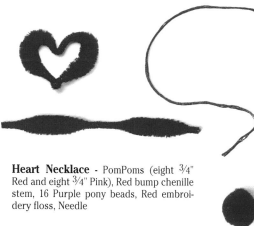

2 - Color Twist

3 - Color Braid

4 - Color Weave

Butterfly - PomPoms (Three 10mm Pink), Chenille stems (Purple bump and Orange 3mm), ¹⁄₄" elastic

Spiral Bracelet - PomPoms (Six 10mm Orange and ¹⁄₂" Yellow), Chenille stems (Two Pink, 1 Purple and 1 Orange 6mm)

Holiday Ornaments

Celebrate the Holidays with quick and colorful ornaments.

Heart - Chenille stems (White 6mm and Red 6mm and 9mm)

Penguin - PomPoms (Black - 1½", 1"; White 5mm), Chenille stems (Red, Orange and White 9mm, White 3mm, Black bump), Red, Orange and White felt, Two 6mm wiggle eyes, Red embroidery floss, Needle

Spiral Christmas Tree - PomPoms (¾" Yellow and twelve 5mm Red), Chenille stems (Green 15mm and Brown 6mm), Red embroidery floss, Needle

Flat Christmas Tree - PomPoms (½" Yellow and five 5mm Red), Chenille stems (Green and Brown 6mm), Red embroidery floss, Needle.

Angel - PomPoms (1½" White, two 5mm Pink), Chenille stems (Pink, Purple and Yellow bump and Gold Glitter bump), 5" of ¾" White lace, Polyester fiberfill, Two 6mm wiggle eyes, Red embroidery floss, Needle

Snowman in Wreath - PomPoms (White 1½", Green eight ¾", Red six 5mm, Black four 3mm), Chenille stems (Black, Red and Orange 6mm), Red and Black felt, Two 6mm Black half round eyes, Red embroidery floss, Needle

Star - PomPoms (five 10mm Green), Chenille stems (Red and Yellow 6mm)

Wreath - PomPoms (8 Green ¾"; 6 Red 5mm; Grey - 1", 10mm; Pink - 5mm; White - 5mm), Chenille stems (Red 6mm and White 3mm), Red, Pink and Grey felt, Two 5mm wiggle eyes, Red embroidery floss, Needle.

Holly - PomPoms (Three ½" Red), Green Foam, Leaf pattern on page 10, Red embroidery floss, Needle

Santa Face - PomPoms (1½" and ½" White, 10mm Red), Chenille stems (White 9mm and Red 6mm), Flesh and White felt, Two 6mm wiggle eyes, Red embroidery floss, Needle

Reindeer - PomPoms (Beige 1½", Brown ¾", Red - six 5mm, 10mm), Brown 6mm chenille stem, Brown Fun Foam, 6mm Black half round eyes, Red embroidery floss, Needle

Garland - PomPoms (White - three 1", twenty-five ½"; Beige - 1", ½"; Brown - 1", 10mm; Grey - 1", 10mm; Red - twenty-seven ½", three 5mm; Pink 5mm), Chenille stems (Brown, Black and White 3mm, Orange Brown, Black, White and Red 6mm), Red, Black, Flesh, Pink and Grey felt, Twelve 5mm wiggle eyes, White string, Needle

Holiday Ornaments

See Santa Table Topper on page 16. You'll love this terrific setting!

Snowman

Here's a wonderful project for the holidays, and it is so simple and fast to make!

Snowman - PomPoms (White - two 2", two 1½", 1", five ¾"; 3 Black, 2 Yellow, 2 Red and 2 Orange 5mm), Chenille stems (Green, Orange, Black and 2 Brown 6mm), Red, Green and White Fun Foam, Black felt, Two 6mm wiggle eyes, Black marker, Pinking scissors

Rainbow Snake

Great fun to make!

Rainbow Snake - PomPoms (Green - 1½", four 1", two 10mm; Red five 1"; Blue five 1"; Orange five 1"; Yellow four 1"), Chenille stems (Dark Blue and Red 6mm), Two 6mm Black half round eyes